A Swaledale Heritage

Susan Haywood

Printed using Garamond font

ISBN: 9798836386009

DEDICATION

To friends in Swaledale, past and present, who
have featured in this book

CONTENTS

ACKNOWLEDGMENTS

To Dr Vicki Bertram and her writing group who encouraged my writing and especially a latent talent for poetical expression. To Jennie-White Cooper for her art work in delineating the illustrated map of Swaledale and its environs. To Juliet Wimshurst for her observations on the history of the Dale. Finally, to my husband, Graham, who has supported my endeavours, persevered in improving the text and correcting my mistakes.

FOREWORD TO THE SECOND EDITION

We arrived in Swaledale just before the foot and mouth crisis in 2001 established its hold in Northern Britain. With our neighbours, we engaged the support of his then Royal Highness Prince Charles to protect Swaledale from contracting the disease. This would have ravaged the hefted flocks and destroyed the centuries old hefting system. An account of our efforts is given in The Hefted Farmer, 2004.

Subsequently I became interested in the history of Swaledale; in particular, the Swaledale sheep which had been bred to establish a wool trade with continental Europe in mediaeval times. The sheep are still regarded for their hardiness and mothering instincts. Alongside this lead mining was carried out until the late 19th century and the local villages took in miners to swell the then population.

The inhabitants of upper Swaledale were a free-thinking non-conformist people and the so called Swaledale Seekers allied themselves with the Quakers. Indeed, I was told by one of the locals farmers that, within living memory, local people had been baptized in the Swale, a rite initiated by St Paulinus in the seventh century.

The Dales people have retained their individuality to this day.

MAP OF BIRKDALE   Not to scale

Roads ___ Tracks --- Bridleway/Droveroad - - - -

To RAVENSEAT

Birkdale
Tarn

TO TAILBRIDGE HILL
& KIRKBY STEPHEN   B6270

Birkdale

Brown Howe

Ellers

Site of
Chapel

Birkdale Beck

demolished
houses

River Swale

Firs

Loanin End
Mine

Stonehouse

Field Houses/Barns

Great Sleddale Beck

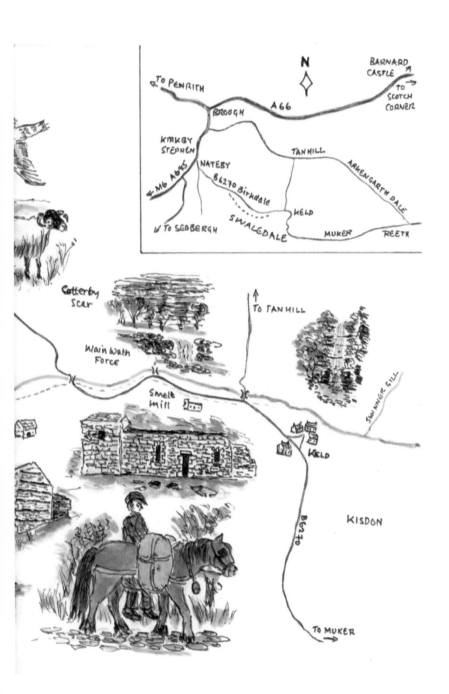

N

BARNARD
CASTLE

TO PENRITH

TO
SCOTCH
CORNER

A66

BROUGH

KIRKBY
STEPHEN

TANHILL

ARKENGARTH DALE

NATEBY

M6 A685

B6270 Birkdale

KELD

TO SEDBERGH

SWALEDALE

MUKER

REETH

Cotterby
Scar

TO TANHILL

Wain Wath
Force

Swinner Gill

Smelt
Mill

Keld

KISDON

B6270

TO MUKER

1
INTRODUCTION

Swaledale is the most northerly and longest of the Dales and arguably the most beautiful.

The dale as we now see it, was carved out after the last ice age, 10,000 years ago, when torrents of melt water poured down hill slicing through carboniferous and sedimentary rocks near Keld. Great ravines were created in this epoch giving rise to the Swale as the *'fast flowing river'*.

The River Swale originates at Dale Head, upper Swaledale in an amphitheatre of hills over 2000ft: Great Shunner fell, Hugh Seat Morville continuing onto High Seat and Mallerstang edge. Subsequently it drops down to Tailbrigg allowing passage from Swaledale into Westmorland before sweeping up again via Coldbergh Edge and onto Nine Standards Rigg over the county boundary. In this wild and beautiful vastness, the rivulets which drain them empty into Sleddale and Birkdale becks which together form the Swale at Dale Head.

Up to the 16th century the length of the Dale down to Richmond was forested by ash, silver birch, oak and hazel. These forests were home to red deer, bears, beaver, wolves and other wild animals. Stone and flint artefacts provide evidence of Neolithic man who more than 2000 years ago roamed these forests. Later, between 700 and 800 AD, Scandinavians arrived from the west (now Kirkby Stephen and Brough) from Westmorland, by way of the pass. They established themselves and gave Nordic place names down dale at Keld (*Kelda-* a spring), Thwaite (*thveit* -a clearing) and Muker (*miorakr-* a narrow field). Personal names also betray their Nordic heritage: - Gunnerside (*Gunners pasture*), Harker, Metcalfe and, most notably, Alder(s)son which is still a mighty clan. Their latter-day descendants possess the upright strong frames, the fair hair and complexions of their Nordic origins.

These Nordic immigrants cleared land for their hefted sheep (that is sheep that clung to their traditional pastures) and so began the system of in-bye walled pastures surrounding the homesteads and leading to the unfenced fell beyond. Sheep farming was supported by the overseas market for wool which was shipped to the continent.

Later still after the Norman conquest, the monks of Rievaulx Abbey were granted manorial rights in upper Swaledale which included hunting, sheep grazing and lead mining, sufficient to establish a small community at Dale head, although nothing now remains of this settlement.

Upper Swaledale was only 20miles from the then Scottish border and so did not escape completely from the different emigrant populations but was constantly harried by invading Scots who carried off their women and cattle. There is a tradition that one such incursion and battle took place at

Brown How, a drumlin found at Dale Head in Birkdale just above Stonehouse farm near Loanin End, and that many combatants were buried here. It is likely that Nine Standards Rigg, the stone-built eminence overlooking Kirkby Stephen served as look-out post against the Scots. Lighting the beacons would have given warning of an imminent incursion to inhabitants of both Westmorland and Cumberland.

Swaledale is known almost uniquely for its lead deposits. Even the Romans were aware of these and, although superficial mining was practised lower down the dale, they never forayed further up the dale, regarding it as wild and dangerous. This was left to a later age and it is thought the demand for lead for the roof tiling of abbeys such as Rievaulx in mediaeval times was met in Swaledale. In the 17th century after the great fire of London, considerable impetus to lead mining was enjoyed due to rebuilding of the city. This encouraged people to settle in Swaledale and work in the mines. Lead mining continued upto the mid-19th century when cheaper Spanish lead flooded the market. This contributed to the collapse of mining in the dales so causing an exodus of the Dales people to work in the fledgling Lancashire cotton industry and even to go overseas to the American colonies.

During this period changes were taking place in the nation as a whole with feuds between religious traditions of the time and the clamour for a prayer book in the vernacular. This was supplied by Thomas Cranmer and soon followed by the King James (Authorised Version) bible. This made for schisms in the church and was led in particular by the men of the North. Swaledale was no exception and a barely literate people formed free thinking sects which has persisted in the Quakers, Methodists and others.

Life in Birkdale, Dale head mirrored the rest of the Dale with an early population expansion due to the combination of farming and lead mining which allowed for an increased population until the mid-19th century. Habitations arose in Ash Gill, Stone house, Firs and Birkdale and smaller dwellings at the head of the dale to make the hamlet of Birkdale, being home to around 100 people. This swelled to more than this due to the advent of daily miners from Keld and beyond.

Employment was guaranteed at Loanin End mine for over 100 years. But the collapse into the 20th century was just as rapid with emigration from the dale when work abated. Within a hundred years, by the mid-20th century the only occupants were, in the main, found in the named farmhouses.

Our own time at Firs began some 50 years later when the only occupied house was our own, with Stonehouse occupied only intermittently and Birkdale in a ruinous state. Our time of living in the Dale is represented by only the smallest movement of the minute hand on the clock of historical time but during which I have become imbued with a sense of the being of the dale, have shared some of its secrets and even perhaps contributed in some small way to its continuing future. We experienced a time of relative turbulence when Foot & Mouth disease (2001) was prevalent in the region and threatened to wipe out the hefted flocks on the moor. Our fight together with that of our then neighbours is told in the book "The Hefted Farmer" which we like to think contributed to saving the unique shepherding practices enjoyed in Swaledale.

We do not know what changes may be brought about in the upper dale either through global warming or projected reafforestation (now known as "rewilding") in the future. We do recognise that currently a balance has been struck between the demands of agriculture, ecology and global requirements. The breeding of low maintenance sheep in a traditional setting perpetuates a way of life which recognises the demands of a non-intensive system which maintains the moorland landscape and yet allows bird species to flourish such as curlew, snipe and lapwing. The boggy moorland supports the growth of sphagnum moss which utilises carbon dioxide as efficiently as trees locking in carbon indefinitely. Indeed, this activity is recognised nationally as an important part of our nation's contribution to lowering greenhouse gases.

After many centuries these Swaledale uplands have achieved a steady state, an ecosystem which has largely evolved and yet remains in keeping with current environmental concerns. It provides employment and recreation for a great many people and it is hoped will be cared for in the future despite all the competing concerns of the modern world.

2
THE LOST HAMLET OF BIRKDALE

Nothing is permanent. Human affairs, illumined by the light of a particular epoch, subside as time moves on. Envisioned over the centuries, the small hamlet of Birkdale in Upper Swaledale rose to a seeming permanence from the 17th to early 19th centuries and then declined into insignificance. Its demise, from being a hill-farming and lead-mining community, was hastened by the collapse of the price of lead on the world market.

Earlier centuries had witnessed a settlement at the origin of the river Swale with reference to a small monastic community in mediaeval times.

This derived probably from the Cistercian monks of Rievaulx Abbey who, as owners of the manors of Upper Swaledale, enjoyed all rights and privileges. Nothing remains of their wood and turf dwellings but they presumably practised some sheep husbandry which was being encouraged down-dale on account of the demand for wool. Venison and other game could be had from the then abundant forests of this region.

Geologic upheavals in early times had resulted in rich veins of lead lying close to the surface. Excavation with picks, coupled with the use of rushing water, could release the lead-bearing ore to those with the persistence to work on such shallow seams. Later, the sinking of deep shafts, coupled with some mechanisation, resulted in the establishment of more permanent mines, of which Loanin End in Birkdale was such a one. At the height of its functioning in the 18th and 19th centuries, mining, coupled with subsistence farming, was able to support up to 20 families, together with the day workers who came up dale from Keld and beyond. The stone-built houses, clustered mainly around the source of the Swale, constituted a small but vibrant community named after one of the tributaries of the Swale: Birkdale. By this time the region, despite its name, "Birch", was largely devoid of trees which had been used to fuel the lead-smelting kilns, or to provide pit props for the mines.

Stonehouse, Firs and Birkdale are the only extant houses at the present time and although these were occupied by farming families as recently as 1930, nowadays they benefit only from tourism and holiday lets. However, before 1900 when the lead industry collapsed, several stone barns which stood on the hillside, Ashgill, Stirkholme and Whamphouse still remain as once-likely dwellings.

It is recorded that in the field adjacent to Stonehouse several more modest dwellings plus a bakehouse stood by the riverside with easy access to Loanin End mine across the river. All traces have disappeared with accounts by a local lady of their clearance by her grandfather early in the 20th century to create more pasture for his livestock. Indeed, much stone was removed from unoccupied dwellings to enhance the houses of those still remaining. There are also in the records accounts of a chapel, and presumably a burial site, but my patient search of the area has not found any signs of such.

This picture of peace and tranquility is deceptive, for before the start of the 20th century, Dalehead was a hive of activity, indeed semi-industrial, in that lead mining with the noise of the water-fed machines lifting the crude ore in buckets, the men descending down into the dark, dank pits, the patient line of ponies their paniers filled with ore fording their way across the river and down the rough track. All this must have made for a lively scene.

For nearly two centuries Birkdale hamlet had provided a good livelihood for upto 150 people until the failure in the late 19th century of the world market in lead. Sheep farming in this inhospitable region was insufficient to provide a living and there was a mass emigration from Swaledale as a whole. The smaller tenants abandoned their homes and land and moved towards the industrial heartlands of Lancashire and Yorkshire. Several families of an enterprising nature migrated to America and records attest to men of Swaledale doing well in mining and farming regions around the Mississippi.

Move forward to the 20th century and the hamlet of Birkdale exists in name only. The few remaining farmsteads no longer serve their former function and the lead mine has long since been abandoned to the elements, remaining only as a few tumbling walls and a deep mine shaft in which shade-loving ferns have found a home.

Impermanence

Time passes, illuminating epochs,

giving a seeming permanence

to human affairs.

Before moving on, sliding into obscurity.

In Swaledale for upwards of two centuries,

the upper dale rang with the clank of water-
fed machines,

lifting buckets of crude lead ore from dank
mines.

The raucous shouts of men's voices,

mellowed by the sonorous bells of jagger
teams,

ferrying their loads down dale.

Before economic forces collapsed men's

livelihoods

and forced their emigration overseas.

Dwellings abandoned, the land reclaimed by
sheep

and the mournful cry of curlew and plover.

Where will Time next illuminate?

Perhaps full circle, with reafforestation

and man's retreat,

to return the wild wood

to that which once it was?

And deer, fox and badger reclaim their
ancient home.

3
SHEPHERDING IN UPPER SWALEDALE:
HEAFS AND HILL FARMS

This valley, or "dale" from its Scandinavian derivation, is unlike anywhere else in England and is reminiscent of the lower slopes of the Swiss mountains: the springy turf sprinkled with wild flowers, the heights rising precipitously from green bottom pastures. This likeness is augmented by the deep glaciated ravine which cuts through the hillside at Keld to expose the tumultuous falls that carry the river Swale down to the flatter plains beyond.

The valley bottoms are divided into small pastures by stone walls which snake up the hillside, before giving way to the untrammelled fells. The alpine character is emphasised by the innumerable stone barns which occupy each field. The stone barns and farmhouses recall their Viking ancestry with their longhouses and separate field barns for wintering stock and the storage of fodder. Their prevalence and longevity would appear unique in England and is evidence of a historical continuity.

Kisdon, Swaledale

The river Swale is the confluence of two becks, Birkdale and Sleddale at Loanin End. Swaledale can be said to be synonymous with its sheep and, though lead mining has sometimes played a close second, for sheer persistence and longevity the sheep have it!

sThe Swaledale breed so designated by genetics and serendipity, has for its qualities become one of the premier breeds in the UK. Furthermore, the site associated with its ascendancy and pre-eminence has come to be recognised as upper Swaledale in that aggregate of smallholdings known as Birkdale at Swalehead.

Stonehouse

Although reduced in occupancy in the 21st century, in the early 20th century it was the farmers living at Stonehouse, The Firs and neighbouring farms, who established their provenance and in 1919-1923 registered these sheep as a distinct breed in the 'Swaledale Sheep breeders Association' recording, maintaining and improving their characteristics for all time.

Hefting

The Swaledale sheep are renowned for their hardiness, strong mothering and territorial instincts. So strong were the latter that the practice of 'heafing' or 'hefting' appeared in which the sheep and their farm are integral to a piece of unfenced fell and have been since time immemorial. (It is thought the Norsemen practised sheep husbandry in their time and that the local sheep were related to the Herdwick Westmorland strain which also possess this strong homing instinct.) The heafs arise beyond the enclosed in-bye fields surrounding the farm and extend onto the unenclosed fell. Each heaf consists of 100 to 120 acres of fell, all with individual names derived from geographical features; for example: Uldale, Coldbergh and Ash Gill. So localised are the heafs that the hefted sheep (100 or so) develop their own individual characteristics over time, which they pass onto their offspring. The contiguity of the heafs meanwhile maintain the integrity of the system and limit any attempt of the sheep to wander.

Map of the Heafs, Upper Swaledale

(by courtesy, The Hefted Farmer)

Whilst the origins of the breed derive their probable descent from the Norse immigrants in 9th and 10th centuries, the perpetuation of the desirable breed type was in the 12th and 13th centuries when the Cistercian monks of Rievaulx Abbey were granted the manorial rights of Upper

Swaledale. It is said that by this time there was a small monastic community in Birkdale by the side of the Swale at Dalehead, although there is now no sign of what would most likely be of timber and earth construction. The abbots encouraged the clearing of sheep walks for the keeping of sheep on the upper fell pastures and established a successful wool trade with the continent of Europe. [

Uldale Hefted Sheep

The graded wool was transported on pack ponies to be shipped from Stockton, York and Whitby to the continent. Thus, after the depredations of the Norman conquest, sheep farming helped bring a living to those who lived in the wilder districts of the Yorkshire dales, which were unsuitable for cereal farming. In these earlier times it was the suitability of the hard-wearing fleece for clothing, rather than for meat, which drove sheep breeding.

It is of interest that on the other side of the Pennines in the 14th century, the characteristics of the Swaledale sheep's wool was deemed eminently suitable for the production of high-quality, hard-wearing tweeds. The Flemish wool manufacturer, John Kemp, brought Flemish weavers to settle in the district around Kendal and established 'Westmorland tweed' which is still produced today. So was established a home market for Swaledale wool as well as for its export.

Foddering, Whiteside Heaf

Thus, the characteristics of the Swaledale breed of sheep has withstood the test of time. Although its wool is less sought after today, the sheep's hardiness and mothering instincts are prized and often used in other cross breeds. Whilst it enjoys its well-deserved reputation at local shows, predominantly the Muker show in September, it is to be hoped that its longevity will persist into the future.

These sheep have their detractors and have been blamed for moorland degradation due to overstocking, but removal of remunerative subsidies has taken care of this because it's no longer viable to have large flocks on the fell. There are those who regard sheep grazing as essentially unnecessary and an unethical use of our moorlands which they say should be turned over to rewilding schemes. I would argue that such ideas are counter-productive, since such overlooks the good that careful grazing has done on these moorlands by the sheep which maintain the balance of grasses and heather. This combination can become overgrown and so discourage nesting birds such as curlew, snipe and grouse. Moreover, the maintenance of the in-bye pastures for the haymaking allows the growth of abundant wild flowers which are such a glory in spring and summer. In such a well-tried ecosystem which benefits man and beast do these upland farms thrive.

We moved to upper Swaledale in the late 20th century and settled in The Firs, an old stone farmhouse at Dalehead, in Birkdale, not far from Stonehouse and Loanin End lead mine.

The Firs

Finally, I witnessed for myself what could have been disaster to the hefted flocks when, in 2001, foot and mouth disease ravaged the country and badly thought-out governmental plans for control of the epidemic sought for the culling of both affected and contiguous farmsteads. These plans were made by those with no experience of hill-farming or the importance of the heafs. If the disease had crossed into Swaledale, which it very nearly did except for the action of local farmers, disaster beckoned. With the timely support of Prince Charles, a disinfection point was established at the Westmorland and Yorkshire county-boundary. As one old farmer said "*If the disease crosses the county boundary it would spread down this narrow dale like the west wind and wipe out all the hefted sheep .. .. and we should never recover*". For once the heafing system is broken it cannot be recovered, built up, as it is for over a thousand years.

We should all be the losers: a loss of the green mosaic of walled fields with their barns leading to the glorious unfenced, heather-covered fells. An ecosystem of carbon retaining peatbogs, unpolluted rivers and the wild life that they support: a precious legacy from our forebears to be held in trust for those who come after.

Vigilance is required more than ever!

Heafs and Hill Sheep

Open moorlands, desolate,

delineated by black peat escarpments

overlain with waving cotton grass.

Unfenced heafs known to ancestral sheep,

Uldale, White Spots Gutter, Crook Syke

Coldbergh and Black Howe,

Middletown and Roberts seat;

barely remembered names

evoking times past.

Mosaic of walled green fields

in valley bottoms,

wrested out by Viking incomers

centuries ago

in Muker, Thwaite and Keld

named villages

remaining so today.

4
Natural History of Upper Swaledale

THE SEASONS

Winter

In winter the treeless moors are lashed by heavy rain or hidden under snow.

Sheep are still retained and foddered on the heafs, although the young stock are sent down to lowland pastures.

Wild life is generally at a low ebb. However, moles make their presence known by their burrowing tunnels throwing up mole hills.

An original acrylic painting by Robin Haywood

Stoats are remarked by a quick glimpse of their elegant form with their characteristic black tipped tail and, in a severe winter, by their white ermine.

The sad corpse of a rabbit with a fatal neck wound is the more usual evidence of a stoat's activity.

But predators are not plentiful as the moors support grouse and gamekeepers are employed to keep down foxes and others.

The red grouse is considered to be our only British game bird and is protected for sport and for the table. It is a rather heavy bird with a cover of rich chestnut feathers and can be seen in small family parties foraging on lower pastures. When startled, the bird emits a sharp staccato cry and flies low and fast across the heather. It competes with sheep, it is said, for the heather shoots on which it feeds. Consequently, the sheep population has been reduced in recent times to assist in the recovery of the red grouse, which was in danger of depletion. It lays upto ten brownish speckled eggs in a scooped-out hollow beneath the heather.

The black grouse, its cousin, is more rare. It is traditionally fond of tree cover and occurs hereabouts on Cotterby Scar, a tree covered limestone outcrop adjacent to the open fell. One of the sights of winter are these birds flying low over a frozen Birkdale Tarn with their characteristic long glide.

Birkdale Tarn in Winter

The male black grouse, or Blackcock, is a very spectacular gentleman with a red flash on his jet-black feathering and his characteristic lyre-shaped tail. In spring, his courting displays known as "lecs" can be seen when several males compete for the attention of the dowdier females.

The pheasant is said to be an introduced species but there is no doubt it has become naturalised and is a common sight in winter bringing a splash of colour to the pastures of the dale.

They live in small mixed flocks of males and

females. Its three-toed prints, with tell-tale marks made by its tail feathers, are conspicuous on snowy ground.

Winter can be glorious.

On occasion when the snow falls and lies for a week or more the countryside is thrown into sharp relief; long icicles hang from banks and the river itself may become partially frozen over. The velvet nights are illuminated by all the stars of the Milky Way. Orion the hunter stalks the Great Bear across the cosmic wastes watched by the shy Pleiades and Cassiopea. Sometimes, Jupiter hangs like a great jewel in the East. Often, the red planet Mars and Venus herself can be seen in all their glory.

Under favourable conditions around the Winter Solstice the northern sky is illuminated by a glow that has nothing to do with pollution but is from the Northern Lights which are themselves sometimes visible.

All these sights were commonplace once but today are only seen in the depths of the countryside having now been drowned out in towns and cities by the harsh fluorescence of modernisation.

We are belittled by this, our imaginations stultified and our place in the cosmos reduced to banality.

Into Spring

Spring comes late to these Northern uplands. The first greening is not seen until mid-April when the flocks return to lamb on their home pastures. From then until mid-May, primroses, violets and wild pansies appear on sheltered banks, colt's foot and celandines too.

Ewes and lambs at Black Howe

By the riverside palm, hazel and alder catkins appear and the blackthorn bursts into bloom.

The tender green of the new-leafed trees holds Spring's advance in suspense as the days lengthen and slowly warm.

Spring returns to Keld

The turn of the year is heralded by the return of the wading birds from sheltered coastal estuaries.

First come the lapwings in ones and twos until one day a cloud of between thirty or forty wheels into view over the top pasture with their characteristic cry of "pee whit, pee whit". They are followed by the curlews making that most evocative long drawn piping call and afterwards, the redshanks and snipe. Indeed, March is borne in by a cacophony of bird calls extending well into the evening and the moors come alive with their music.

These birds make their nests on the ground of the high pastures and on the moorland itself. By late March it is not uncommon to come across a shallow nest of loosely woven grass containing as many as four eggs. The eggs are generally green coloured, flecked with brown. Great care is needed during the breeding season when one walks over the moors so as not to step onto the camouflaged eggs.

Lapwings nest

The numbers of wading birds that frequent these northern hills during the breeding season has led to them being designated as Sites of Special Scientific Interest (SSSI) which put restrictions on the use and management of these uplands. For example, peat, once the staple fuel for burning in the grates of the cottages, can no longer be removed from the peat bogs. Also, the dykes which once drained the bogs have been filled in so that the whole land remains wet with the sphagnum mosses, which eventually become peat.

Waders are by no means the only birds. Down by the river banks the oyster catcher, a flamboyant black and white bird with a distinctive piping call and sporting red legs, is a fairly recent arrival. A pair of herons can be seen winging a slow and graceful flight up and down the upper dale. More modestly the dipper a small brown and white bird patrols its designated patch of river announcing itself quite cheerily to those who might be about to come too close. In the early morning the ring ouzel vies with its cousin, the blackbird, for supremacy. It sports a striking white collar and sings loudly from a leafless tree emulating, but not surpassing, the blackbird.

The song thrush is occasionally seen although his cousins the mistlethrush and fieldfare are frequent winter visitors descending in flocks on the waterlogged pastures. A diverse collection of other birds including finches, meadow pipits and wagtails, including the rather rare yellow wagtail. The wren, our smallest bird, is plentiful but rather shy and one Spring day we were alerted by strange musical pipings which seemed to fill the air and were revealed as a family of fledging wrens who had just left their nest and were filling the air with their song.

Spring is not really here until the arrival of the swallows and on the first of May the first swallows arrive to make a reconnaisance of the barns their habitual nesting sites. Some years too, the house martins make their carefully constructed nests under the eaves of the houses or in the recessed shelter of the windows; nests which can be reused year after year.

But these are not the only birds. The fells are also home to raptors or birds of prey, among which are counted the merlin, the hen harrier, the peregrine falcon and the more common buzzard.

Spring into Summer

Late spring and early summer sees the full blooming of the meadow and wayside flowers. The sheep are removed from the lower pastures to graze on the fells and the meadows allowed to grow for hay time.

Hayfield in bloom

Hay meadow filled with buttercups, Swaledale

Grants have been awarded to preserve the old hay meadows and to restrict the time of cutting the grass for hay. This enables the flowers to pollinate and for the seed to set so that the meadows can bloom in the following year. Making hay, rather than silage, allows for all this and for the chicks of wading birds to mature and leave their nests.

For a time, mid-August is summer's fulfillment: nests are emptying and fledglings are trying out their wings; swallows and martins dive and sweep across the skies; tits, chaffinches and charms of goldfinches visit the thistle heads. On the pastures lapwings gather in large flocks; oyster catchers and curlews all get ready to leave in autumn for the estuaries, their winter feeding grounds.

Rowan trees are filled with unripe berries, as are the rose and sloe. On the moors the heather is a drift of purple haze; the air is heady with its honeyed smell.

And so to autumn

The trees in the maple grove turn to flame incorporating red and gold in their painted leaves.

A grove of Canadian Maples – unusual in Swaledale

Elderberries droop wine-dark from thicket stems and dark-purple sloe berries can be found down-dale. Hazelnuts, acorns and mahogany horse chestnuts lie in profusion on the ground where they have fallen from the overladen trees.

Slowly and, seemingly, reluctantly the trees shed their leaves and their bare branches are exposed to the stormy skies.

November and December are grey months waiting on the winter solstice when the sun leaves the deepest valleys in shadow and the frost never thaws.

5

MEN OF LEAD

Lead-mining in Upper Swaledale

Pack ponies carried their loads of lead ore along the rough track from Loanin End lead mine, past Stonehouse and The Firs, farms in Birkdale, upper Swaledale. The team then continued on its way to the smelt mill in Keld by following the river to meet the drovers' teams carrying coal from the Tan Hill pits via Ravenseat and the limestone outcrop, Cotterby Scar. In the mid-18th century, the rough road down from upper Swaledale was a busy place with a two-way procession of pack ponies carrying ore, coal or provisions up and down the dale.

Keld Side Mill, Cotterby Scar

The demand for lead was very great. London was being completely rebuilt after the Great Fire in 1666; large manor houses were being built throughout the country and Rievaulx Abbey took advantage of the available lead for its roofing.

Lead mining at Birkdale was initiated in the early 18th century when two shafts were dug at High and Low Birkdale. A vein of lead ore was discovered at Loanin End and the direction of the vein was exploited by the miners along horizontal levels, the gaping holes of which can be seen on the adjacent hillside. These later becoming available for drainage down-stream.

The ore was dug out using short-handled picks and manually loaded into buckets. These were originally lifted out of the mine by hand; later, by using a horse-drawn chain of buckets; and later still, by water wheels and steam engines.

The ruins of Loanin End mine still persist in Birkdale. The buildings, such as they are, comprise an engine-house by the side of a deep shaft lined by stone, covered now with ferns and mosses and falling deep into the earth some 150 feet or more.

Engine House, Loanin End Lead Mine

Loanin End Lead Mine

This shaft is now covered by cast-iron pipes, the remains of a water conduit to bring water from Birkdale tarn to power the lifting gear. They have been placed over the shaft to prevent the fall of unwary sheep.

Birkdale tarn is the enlargement of a small natural tarn on the heights above Birkdale with extensive stonework to the west of the tarn. The stonework served to raise the level of the waters and to help form an in-take to the water conduit serving Loanin End. A four-mile water race had been dug from Ulldale fells to tap the many water courses and entered the north side of the tarn at 1600ft. The race fell about 50 feet over its length. Its construction was a tremendous undertaking in those early times.

Birkdale Tarn, Intake

When one gazes down the shaft at Loanin End, no sign of how the miners descended can be discerned but the sound of running water is a reminder of just how wet these mines could be and, as such, a constant hazard to the lead-mining. Working conditions were cramped, wet and cold for the men working the mines but the constant demand for lead and the perennial promise of a 'lucky strike' spurred on these hardy men.

The lead ore, prior to being loaded and carried down the dale, was first worked in nearby 'bouse pits' close to the mine head. The 'bouse', an amalgamation of lead ore, rock and mineral waste, or 'gangue', was separated into its components by pick and hand. The ore was then washed before loading onto the pack ponies. The destination was the smelting mill in Keld but prior to this being built, it is likely that the smelting took place nearby the mine itself in a bouse pit. The pit would be packed with combustible material from the still abundant woods and set alight. The molten lead would then be poured into moulds and allowed to set.

Bouse Pits, Loanin End Lead Mine

Who were these early miners and where did they come from? Evidence from early 19th century census returns shows that the populations of Keld and Muker doubled to over a thousand from the mid-18th to 19th centuries and that a large proportion gave 'miner' as their occupation. As this was not accompanied by an increase in building it must be assumed that these itinerant miners lodged with the indigenous population.

In addition, the hamlet of Birkdale, itself by Loanin End mine, had a population occupying twenty houses, with the nucleus by the Swale in Birkdale on the site of the old monastic community. Within living memory, a family of ten lived by the engine-house at Loanin End. There was also a bakehouse which would have served the community. Those houses were levelled towards the end of the 19th century when the industry declined. Other dwellings were on the hillside across the river from Stonehouse. Ashgill, Stirkholme and Whamp house were occupied from the 17th century onward by a family, the Harkers, which progressed from husbandman to yeoman - evidence of relative prosperity in those times. These small farms were either erased or converted into barns in the 19th century when the Birkdale population declined.

Aside from these relatively settled families in Birkdale who combined working in the lead mines with their small holdings, the work force at Loanin End consisted largely of itinerants who either lodged in nearby Keld and Muker or locally near the mine. There is evidence that Stonehouse took in numbers of these men.

For the men who tramped daily from the local

villages, life must have been tough. They had a two-mile trudge to and from the mine, starting out and returning in darkness in winter and often in inhospitable conditions. They then had to descend down the mine for a six hours or more working day. Many of them increased their weekly wage by some prospecting of their own, seeking out new veins of lead on the surface away from the mine. This was deemed lawful if not particularly remunerative since the proceeds were often spent on drink!

Lead-mining grew in importance throughout the 17th and 18th centuries; and well into the mid to late 19th century when the industry suddenly declined due to the import of cheaper lead from the Spanish mines. This event was devastating. Lead-mining had provided work and subsistence for around four thousand people over more than two centuries. The cheap imports made the Swaledale lead commercially non-viable and so provoked a mass emigration of people to the mills of Lancashire and beyond.

In upper Swaledale, Birkdale as a community remains in name only, leaving the only habitable houses as Stonehouse, The Firs , Birkdale and Ellers. None of which is no longer in full time occupancy. Evidence of lead-mining remains: the treeless moors, the piles of rubbish and spoil from the pits and the gashed hillsides. Time has healed to some extent, though the tree cover and the forest denizens, the great herds of deer are no more. The sheep have reclaimed their land.

Jagger Pony

Jagger ponies

Jang, jang, jang the sonorous sound,

as the bell-mare guides her team

of sturdy Galloways along rough tracks,

laden with lead ore from the mine

to smelting mill down dale.

Jagger-ponies, whose humble lives,

yet played their part

in roofing Rievaulx Abbey,

And fire-torn London town.

A lesson how the least of us

contribute to the living tapestry,

Of time and place.

Loanin End

Look close: a rough construct of stone,

hostage to the harsh winters of these
uplands.

Two hundred years ago a thriving noisy
mill,

powered by water to lift the leadstone

from the deep bowels of the earth.

The shaft, one hundred and fifty feet falls
to watery depths,

down which men toiled,

now host to green moss and ferns.

Covered by heavy metal pipes along which
once water flowed

from upland tarn to work the mill.

Times past, this mill supported three hundred
souls,

who lived in Birkdale hamlet.

But times have changed,

and the mineral wealth, lead sought since
Roman times,

now is no more.

The land divested of its forest trees,

used as fuel to melt the ingots,

reverts to pasturage for sheep.

A sign of the despoiling of the planet - our
only home?

6
MEN OF STONE

The mosaic of grey, stone walls that pattern the hillside like a spider's web and snake up the fells in Swaledale are unlike anywhere else in England, so little do they resemble the hedges of more southerly counties. In common with the hedges, they provide a delineation of fields and shelter for stock.

The enclosure of pieces of land or fields arose with the Norse invaders who on arriving in the stony landscape in upper Swaledale felled the trees around their dwellings and cleared the boulders, thus making enclosures to protect and prevent their cattle and flocks from straying, the so-called 'garths'. The enclosures multiplied and enlarged over time, frequently containing a stone barn for the holding of hay and wintering of stock. This was very typical of their Norse heritage and this appearance on the steep hillsides of upper Swaledale led to them being described as an English Tyrol. The work was over many generations and continued as conditions allowed. But in the early 19th century, the Enclosure Act put an end to this gradual development as the straighter walls which run up to the edge of the fells testify.

Dry stone walling was, and still is, a well-honed skill passed on from father to son on the farms but also still employing some professional stone-wallers who are in much demand. New walls are much less frequent nowadays but gaps in walls made by enterprising sheep, or by the harsh weather, are relatively common and must be repaired. Essentially, the walls are made without mortar which is why they are called 'dry stone walls'. They must be strong to withstand gale force winds whilst acting as wind breaks and shelter.

Dry stone walling in Birkdale

The wide base of two feet or more must support a wall four to five feet high. The wall is formed from two faces of carefully placed stones with the centre gap being filled by random stone or infill. The rule for building the external faces is that each stone shall sit on two stones and two stones shall sit on one stone. The stones are chosen so that each row, or course, is level. This allows a 'through-stone' to be placed every two to three courses up. The through-stone goes across both faces to bind the two together and, at the same time, forming a solid base on which the new few courses of stone might be built. The whole is topped-off by a similar, but smaller, through-stone which prevents rain from entering the centre of the wall. A single layer of closely-fitting coping stones finishes everything off.

An experienced waller develops a keen eye for the right stone and can pick out from the pile of stones, a stone of just the right width and height needed to form the row. The stone might require some trimming with a stone-hammer, but this is very infrequent because the stone is almost invariably just the right size. The completed wall is strong, absorbing the force of the wind due to its porous nature. Indeed, such is the skill required that competitions are regularly held and keenly supported in the countryside.

Barns and Bridges

In the mid-19th century, building with stone in the form of stone barns and bridges reached their apotheosis. John Alderson Scott of Stonehouse married a stone mason's daughter and, before he was forty years old, had made his fortune in London before returning to his native farm as a master builder. He set to work remodelling Stonehouse before pulling down small stone dwellings in Birkdale which he transformed into handsome stone barns. The same techniques used in the dry-stone walling have been applied, foregoing the use of mortar as used in modern buildings. The 'through' stones shown in the barns are so angled to allow the drainage of rain water from the building. Each stone forming the wall is, itself, pitched to allow the water to drain off.

Ashgill Barn

He completed this transformation with three stone bridges spanning the Swale from Stonehouse to Hoggarths farm and bearing the date stones 1840.

Stonehouse Bridge

The arch of the bridge was initially built onto a wooden framework which was later removed on completion. Otherwise, the bridge building used essentially the same techniques aforementioned although some mortar is apparent in more recent applications.

Low Bridge, Cotterby Scar

It is tribute to the extraordinary craftmanship and skill of these builders in upper Swaledale nearly two hundred years ago that these structures have withstood the onslaughts of weather and time to give us lasting monuments of such beauty and durability in this remote dale.

Men of Stone

Hewn out from quarry side

and shaped to fit the hand.

Placing interlocking pieces

giving substance to an idea,

of barn and bridge or wall.

Utilitarian in concept,

beautiful in realization,

as a Michelangelo

in dream for humankind.

7
PEOPLE OF FAITH:
RELIGIOUS LIFE IN UPPER SWALEDALE

Keld: *A Thin Place.*

Latterly, I have become aware that the Swale, the *'fast flowing river'*, can be regarded as a metaphor for our own lives: embedded in, but travelling through, time onto an, as yet, unknown future. There are places where it seems that an intersection can take place in this continuum: the so-called *'thin places.* Keld is regarded as one such locally, where past and present may interpenetrate. Keld, (from the old Norse for 'spring') lies on the course of the river Swale where, at the end of the last Ice Age, the melting ice carved out a huge ravine in the hillside allowing torrents of water to change course, isolating Kisdon Hill as an island. Whether Keld's location at the focus of a great geological event or from its history of hosting non-Conformist preachers accounts for its reputation as a thin place none can tell.

Howsoever that may be, the Swale has had a further function from very early times: that of the cleansing of souls.

An old sheep farmer who had once lived at Stonehouse near Dalehead where I then lived, told me that he and his forebears before him had been baptised in the Swale at this very site, by full immersion; a practice initiated by St Paulinus in the 7th century AD.

Pope Gregory had sent his bishop, Paulinus, to convert the heathen people of the North. Paulinus had set up camp at the riverside by, what is now, the village of Catterick near Richmond, North Yorkshire. It is recorded that he baptised people in their thousands!

Possibly there is some exaggeration here, but his name still lingers on in the village as 'St Paulinus

Crescent'. Also, according to my farmer-friend, the Swale received the appellation the Holy River or the River Jordan of the North after Paulinus' baptisms.

It seems strange that this custom still persisted into the 20th century - well over a thousand years – but has since, probably, died out. The old man, himself, who told me this story died some years ago and no one lives at Stonehouse any more.

Free Thinkers of Swaledale

The inhabitants of upper Swaledale are a self–reliant, feisty set of people. Being independent husbandmen, yeoman farmers, they pledged allegiance to no man. Not for them the serf-overlord relationship that so often oppressed the inhabitants of more southerly regions. They can be good neighbours but also bitter opponents when in conflict. They have always eked out an often frugal existence with subsistence farming on the poor cold land they farmed, supplementing their income by lead mining.

Although often far from schools and the so-called benefits of civilised society this did not prevent them from deeper enquiry into the meaning of life. Once Henry VIII had loosed the established Catholic church from its authoritarian hold after the Reformation, followed by the translation of the Prayer book into English and, later, the Bible into the vernacular, people could access for themselves the Word of God and they took even more control over their own lives. Swaledale was a hot bed of non-conformism: A rough, free-thinking people, often illiterate but fired by Cranmer's recent translation of the prayer book, there arose sects such as the Seekers or Quakers; the Inghamites; and followed later by the Wesleyans and Congregationalists.

The Swaledale Seekers (1650) arose in the early 17th century but were quite quickly absorbed into George Fox's *Seekers after Truth* in 1652. Such sects quickly dispensed with clergy and ritual, so much so, that between 1662 to 1682 the *Society of Friends,* or *Quakers,* as they became to be called, were a proscribed sect, liable to heavy fines or imprisonment.

Records show that one such Simon Harker, yeoman farmer of Birkdale, a tributary of the Swale, one of the original Seekers, travelled to Low Row for meetings with like-minded fellows. It is remarkable that this barely literate farmer who lived far out at the upper end of the dale, with such knowledge as he had gleaned from itinerant preachers, whose days would be long and hard should show such dedication to his new-found religion. Simon would travel along rough tracks walking or on horseback the twelve miles or so down-dale to Low Row where at one such meeting in 1670 records have it that he was *'distrained of a brass pot in lieu of a fine.'*

In these years, undeterred, the Quakers met in lonely places to worship. One such recorded meeting place was in Swinnergill high in the fells above Keld. Swinnergill Kirk, as it became known, was accessed from a steep ravine along a river bed ending in a waterfall. Here they held their services with a lookout on the nearby fell who would raise the alarm if danger presented itself, whereupon the congregation would hide in a cave behind the waterfall until the danger was gone.

We don't know whether Simon was one of these people attending the Kirk, but I would like to think he was. Apart from this, records say he died in 1673 and *'was buried in his own ground, Birkdale'*. What a man! Not for him to be buried in church or chapel-blessed ground but in the land that had nurtured him. To him this was Holy ground. I have looked many times around his erstwhile farm but on the rough fellside there is no apparent site of his internment.

After 1682 the act was repealed by the Act of Toleration and Quakers and others, if licensed, could worship as they would. Those who followed were no less sincere but did not have the hardships encountered by those early 'free spirits' as I like to think of them.

I also like to think that such free spirits, often rough and untutored, live on in special places, these so called 'thin places', where they and their message to us can be accessed to those with time to listen.

Swinnergill Kirk

Embedded in, but travelling through

time's continuum;

an intersection can occur

A *'thin place'*

when past and present interpenetrate

or slip between?

Keld is such a *place*,

on a geological fault line,

when ice-age melt

carved a deep ravine in the hillside.

A place of pilgrimage to hear

the Word of God preached

to a rough untutored people.

High in the Fells in Swinnergill Kirk,

a message still reverberating from this *thin place*.

Swinnergill Kirk

8
EPILOGUE

Free Spirits

Lonely places are their birthing ground,

free spirits who listen to the word of God.

untethered by religion or creed.

A message to the heart

For all to hear who will.

They have no time or place

But occupy the 'in between'

The *thin places* of the world,

accessible to all who ponder

Life's meaning.

Bibliography

The Hefted Farmer by Susan Haywood and
Barbara Crossley
Published by Hayloft Ltd.
ISBN-13: 9781904524205

A Dales Heritage by Marie Hartley and Joan
Inglby
Published by The Dalesman Publishing Company
Ltd. ISBN-13: 9780852067055

Swaledale by Ella Pontefract (in collaboration
with Marie Hartley)
Published by J.M. Dent & Sons Ltd.
ISBN-13: 9781870071192

Muker: The Story of a Yorkshire Parish by
Edmund Cooper
Published by Hayloft Publishing Ltd.
ISBN-13: 9781904524779

ABOUT THE AUTHOR

Susan Haywood is a retired Veterinary Pathologist who spent her professional life at Liverpool University. Subsequently she has lived in Swaledale, North Yorkshire and chronicled the effects of the Foot and Mouth Disease epidemic of 2001 in **The Hefted Farmer** published in 2004/2005.

Latterly she has become interested in the history of Upper Swaledale with an emphasis on the lead mining, stonework and farming activities which have characterized the dale and are the subject of this book.

ABOUT THE ILLUSTRATOR

Jenny White-Cooper is a sign writer and calligrapher who lives in Kirkby Stephen. She is also the illustrator for The Hefted Farmer

AFTERWORD

I was honoured when Susan asked me to help with the publication of this book because it enabled me to read her words and poetry. It was clear from the start that this wasn't a simple historical account of Upper Swaledale, but an expression of her love for the dale, the environment and those peoples that had helped form the dale.

Susan is a world-class veterinary pathologist who has an abiding love of animals and all things natural. She bought The Firs when she was still working at Liverpool University, but soon had her two Fell Pony mares stabled there. From then on, she introduced a small flock of rare North Ronaldsay sheep and, when she retired from the University to live full-time at Firs, expanded her small herd of Fell Ponies to five, the breed being on the endangered list, Unfortunately, she lost a further three to grass-sickness disease.

Although she was an 'in-comer', a role that would normally take several generations before one became a Dalesman or Daleswoman, she was immediately welcomed by George and Mabel Calvert, local farmers of Hoggarts, and made to feel part of the Dale.

However, it was her work in trying to get the government to see sense over its mis-handling of the Foot and Mouth Disease epidemic in 2001 – contacting the Chief Scientist and even Prince Charles in her fight to prevent the disease from spreading into Swaledale - that made her a vital part of the community. All of this, of course, is described in her book, 'The Hefted Farmer'.

But life in the Dales is hard and The Firs is a quarter of a mile from the road up a steep hill. I had problems with my heart at the time, so regrettably we had to leave to live in Kirkby Stephen. Friends from the Midlands took over the North Ronaldsay sheep; the ponies went to live on Stainmore with another friend. But Susan's heart has never left Upper Swaledale and this book is an expression of her love for all that is there.

Graham Haywood

Printed in Great Britain
by Amazon